INTRODUC
How to play your kalimba

STANDARD 10-NOTE KALIMBA IN C SCALE

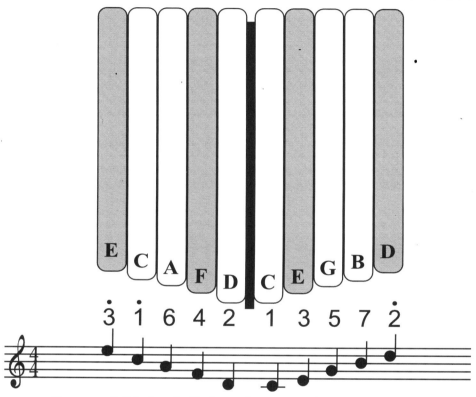

On most 8-10-tine kalimbas, the center tine will be a C note.

STANDARD 17-NOTE KALIMBA IN C SCALE

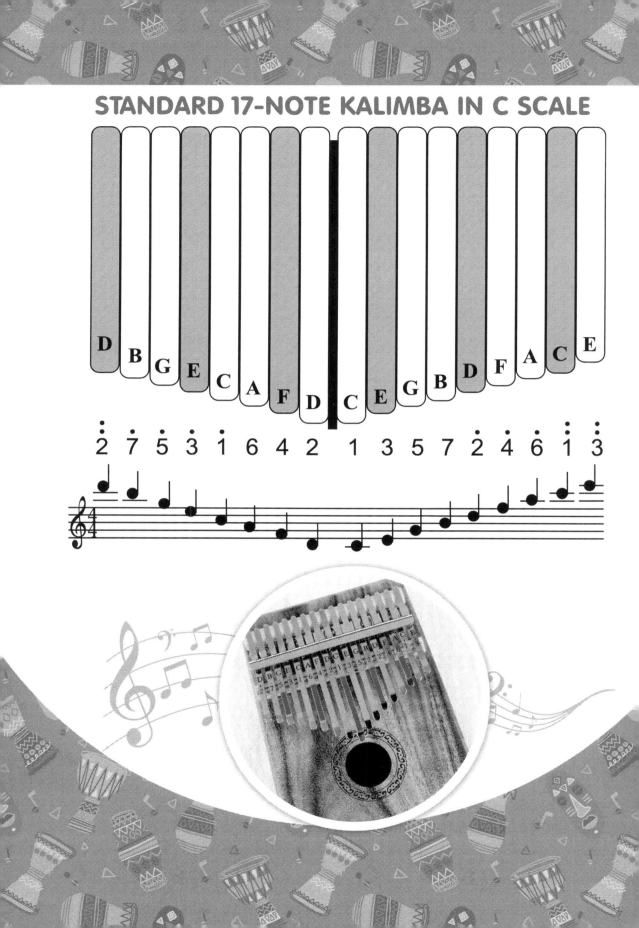

TUNING

If you want good sound, you must tune the keys. You can either use an entity tuner, or you can download a tuner app from your mobile phone. Android System app: gstrings, VITALtuner, Cleartune, and iStrobosoft.

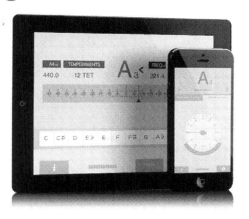

Note: Sometimes the tuner is not sensitive to the keys in the high-pitched position. There may be resonance when you first start playing. Press the keys nearby softly, and then tune your kalimba.

HOW TO HOLD AND PLAY YOUR KALIMBA

- Hold the kalimba with your your thumb on the keys and your other fingers on the side.
- Using your nails to strike the keys will minimize finger pain and make the sound more crisp.
- Use your middle finger to cover the hole on the back to create a WAH sound.
- Train your thumb to move easily between all the keys on each side.

KtabS is a music notation system which was written especially for the kalimba. You can find this in most places and this notation can easily be read. However, we suggest that the easiest way to begin is to play with the letter notes in our book.

Each tab should match the number of tines on your kalimba. For example, if your kalimba has 8 tines, you need to search for "8-note kalimba tabs."

Our sheet music is not for a specific kalimba, but it is universal and suitable for 8-17 note kalimbas.

The modern kalimba usually has enlarged numbers and letters representing the name of the notes. The standard 17 Note Kalimba contains 3 octaves:
1) a full 2nd small octave,
2) a 3rd small octave, and
3) 3 notes from the 4th small octave.

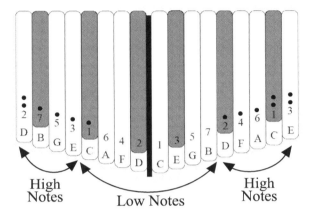

The 2nd small octave goes from C4 to C5 and is depicted in our sheet music as simple numbers. The notes from the 3rd small octave have numbers with one dot above each number. The 3 notes from the 4th small octave - C6, D6, and E6 - are depicted by numbers with two dots above them.

The kalimba or mbira is a traditional and typical African instrument. But the African songs here are written using European notation, and we should understand that songs cannot be written as authentically as the music is played in its original form. Since African music assumes improvisation and variation, we recommend using this sheet music only as a guide. The most important thing is to listen and repeat the recordings linked to the QR code. Follow the link and listen to the rhythm before beginning to play.

Attention: Songs have been transposed for a diatonic range.
Some melodies might be changed and simplified.

Contents

* An indication of the country of origin is an approximation, because many traditional cultures cross current national borders.

Welcome Song*

Song from Uganda

I'm so ex - ci - ted on top of the
moun - tain I feel a joy down in my
heart, That's why I'm sing - ing and
dan - cing, You are wel - come with our view of the
stars, You are wel - come with our view of the stars.

* Songs from the same country have similar patterns

1

Obwisana

Song from Ghana

O - bwi - sa - na sa na - na, o - bwi - sa - na sa;

O - bwi - sa - na sa na - na, o - bwi - sa - na sa.

L'abe igi orombo

Song from Nigeria

Do Do Ki Do

Song from Cameroon

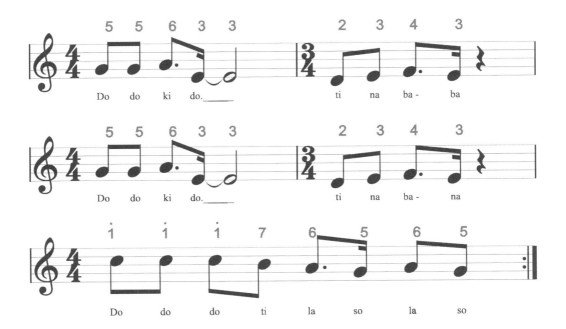

Plouf Tizen Tizen

Song from Algeria

Sansa Kroma

Song from Ghana

Siyanibingelela*

Song from South Africa

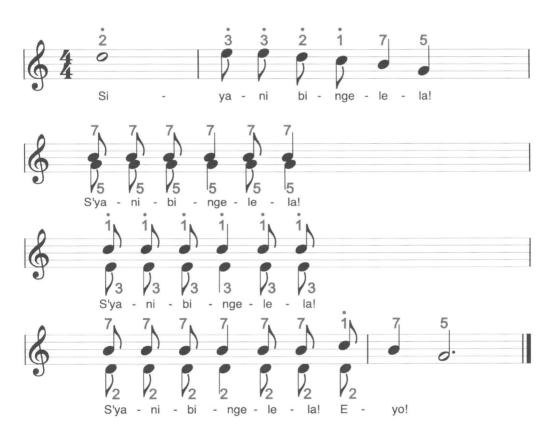

* Song for two instruments. You can play by one.
  Just choose the line you want to play.
  Or try to play with two fingers.

7

Atadwe

Song from Ghana

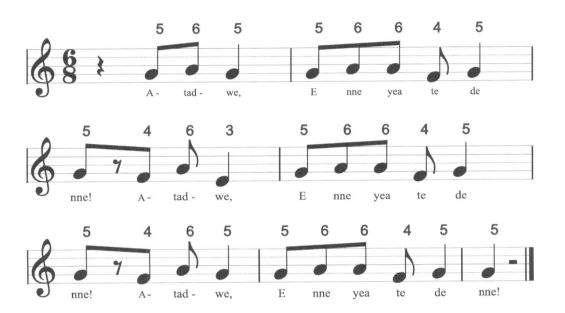

Stick Passing Song

Song from Uganda

Come chil-dren, come chi-dren, come play as we pass the stick, Dan dah ran do, Dan dah ran do Dan dah ran do. Dan dah ran do, Dan dah ran do, Dan dah ran do, Dan dah ran dao. dan dah ran do, Come

A Ram Sam Sam

Song from Morocco

Askari Eee

Song from Tanzania

Coco Laye-Laye

Song from Congo

Kotiko

Song from Congo

Umele

Song from South Africa

Wa Wa Wa

Song from Congo

Zomina

Song from South Africa

Sindi

Song from Burkina Faso

Sélinguenia

Song from Kenya

Before Dinner

Song from Congo

First we go to hoe our gar-den Ya ya ya ya, Next we car-ry jugs of wa-ter, Ya ya ya ya, Then we pound the yel-low corn, Ya ya ya ya, Then we stir our pots of mush, Ya ya ya ya, Now we eat, come ga-ther round the camp-fire Ya ya ya ya

Shosholoza

Song from South Africa

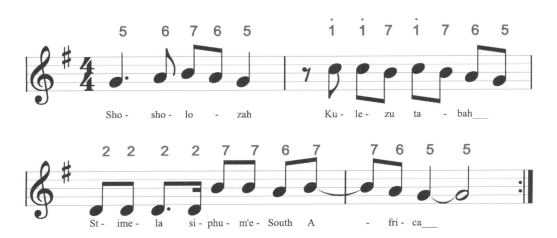

Banaha

Song from Congo

Manamolela

Song from South Africa

Che Che Koolay

Song from Ghana

Kanzenzenze

Song from Congo

Zimbole*

Song from South Africa

*Song may not have originated in Africa, but has been modified

Banuwa

Song from Liberia

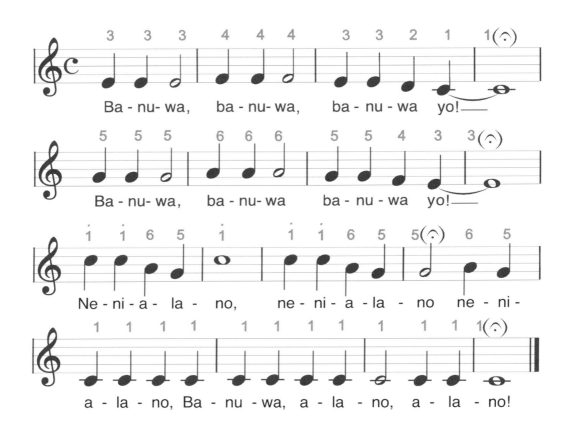

Funga Alafia

Song from Ghana

Mayo Nafwa

Song from Zambia

Siyahamba*

Version 1

Song from South Africa

* Presumably, the song was written by Andries Van Tonder.
  However, it may have been modified from a Zulu folk song

30

Siyahamba

Version 2

Song from South Africa

Eh Soom Boo Kawaya

Song from Nigeria

Bebe Moke

Song from Congo

Be - be mo - ke, na - ni a - be - ti yo,

Lo - ba na gna, ngai pe na - zon - gi - sa.

Mba-la mo - su - su o - tu - ta - ni na

mur ya nda_____ ko.

Achta ta ta ta ta

Version 2   Song from Morocco

Made in the USA
Middletown, DE
17 April 2021